☆ **MASQUERADE** ☆

CRAZY
CREATIONS

ACKNOWLEDGMENTS

MASQUERADE: CRAZY CREATIONS was produced by
Fernleigh Books of 61A Southbury Road, Enfield, Middlesex, EN1 1PJ.

First published in Great Britain by Heinemann Library,
Halley Court, Jordan Hill, Oxford OX2 8EJ,
a division of Reed Educational and Professional Publishing Ltd.
Heinemann is a registered trademark of Reed Educational & Professional Publishing Limited.

OXFORD MELBOURNE AUCKLAND KUALA LUMPUR SINGAPORE IBADAN NAIROBI
JOHANNESBURG GABORONE PORTSMOUTH NH (USA) CHICAGO

British Library Cataloguing in Publication Data
Russon, Jacqueline
Crazy creations. – (Masquerade)
1. Children – Costume – Juvenile literature 2. Handicraft – Juvenile literature
I.Title
646.4'78'06

ISBN 0 431 03587 3

Designer: Gail Rose
Photographer: Steve Gorton
Editor: Louise Pritchard
Illustrator: Mary Hall
Make-up, hair, costumes: Jacqueline Russon

03 02 01 00 99
10 9 8 7 6 5 4 3 2 1

Printed in Hong Kong

The author and Fernleigh Books would like to thank
Rodwins of Southgate for all their help in supplying dancewear and materials.

We would particularly like to thank all the children for their help and patience:
Edward, Samson, Verity, Abigail, Phoebe, Ifalaise, Tom, Alex, Alex, Hannah, Sarah, Ricky and Sophie.

☆ MASQUERADE ☆
CRAZY CREATIONS

Jacqueline Russon

Heinemann

MATERIALS AND TIPS

Dressing up can give you hours of fun and is especially satisfying if you have made the costume yourself. You may be going to a fancy-dress party or just want to dress up for fun. Whatever the reason, you will find an exciting costume in this book to suit the occasion. The illustrated step-by-step instructions are easy to follow. Take care where you see this symbol

[X] and ask an adult to help you.

MATERIALS

Material is often cheapest in local markets but most department stores stock a good variety. Look in charity and second-hand shops for old curtains and clothes, or remnants of material that you could use. If you cannot find the exact material suggested for a costume in this book, or do not like the colour, use a different one. Have fun adapting a costume to use something that you can find.

Always buy foam and wadding for stuffing from a reputable store. You must use flame-retardant foam and safety-approved wadding for stuffing costumes.

TRIMMINGS

You can use lots of different things for trimmings. Save anything you think might be useful – bright buttons, gold braid, ribbons, wrapping paper and cardboard boxes.

Jumble sales and charity shops are good hunting grounds for that special finishing touch. Otherwise, look in material shops or the haberdashery department of any big store. And remember, go wild and improve or change anything you like.

CRAFT MATERIALS

There are many craft materials on the market, such as card, felt and crêpe paper. Large craft shops will have a good stock. Tell the assistant why you want something and he or she will help you find the most suitable material for the job.

The following abbreviations are used for quantities in this book:
sq. cm = square centimetres
sq. m = square metres

PAINTS

Use non-toxic sprays that are specially designed for craft use. Always read the instructions before you use them, and spray only outside or in a well-ventilated area. Water-based acrylic paint is the best to use for costumes, or ordinary poster paints. These are available from all good art shops.

MAKE-UP

All the faces in this book are painted using water-based face paints. These can be bought from most toy or craft shops.

There are also specialist make-up and costume shops that stock a wide range of colours and effects. Some shops will sell by mail-order too. If you are in doubt about the paints you have, ask at a specialist shop.

Make-up is a very simple, but effective way to change your appearance. Follow the tips given here for the best results:

1 *Use only products that are designed for use on the skin, and are of the approved safety standard.*

2 *In case you are allergic to face paints, try them first on your arm.*

3 *Use a slightly damp sponge to apply the base colour.*

4 *Use make-up or soft art brushes to paint in lines and features.*

5 *Use your fingers to make wider stripes, patterns and markings.*

6 *Take great care not to get the paints in your eyes and mouth.*

HEAD CASES

Get all boxed up to go out in one of these crazy creations. You can adapt them and dress up as a different box if you like. Why not try a computer or a radio.

HAIR TIPS
Put gel on your hair. For the diver, brush it out at angles to make it look as if you were underwater.

For the TV newscaster, brush it down with a centre parting.

AQUARIUM
YOU WILL NEED: Cardboard box that fits over your head; silver paint; blue paint; other bright paints; silver card; yellow card; glue; red and green pipe-cleaners; scissors; shells.

TV SET
Stick down the flaps of a box. Cut a hole in the bottom for your head and one in the front for a screen. Cover the TV in sticky-back plastic. Use black card and white corrugated paper for speakers, and bottle tops for knobs. Make an aerial from a plastic bowl painted silver and silver pipe-cleaners. Stick a picture on the back.

NEWSCASTER COSTUME TIPS

Wear a white shirt and jacket with a bright tie. Push a flower or handkerchief into your pocket. Wear what you like from the waist down. It would be fun to wear a sports kit to contrast with the smart top half. If you don't usually wear spectacles, wear some without lenses or make some out of pipe-cleaners.

1 Cut off the top flaps of a box. Cut out the sides and the front, leaving a 3 cm edge all around. Cut a hole in the base for your head. Paint the outside of the box silver and the inside blue.

2 Cut some fish shapes from silver card and paint on scales and fins. Stick the fish to the back of the tank. Cut some yellow card with a wavy edge to look like sand and stick this inside the box at the bottom.

3 Make some curly seaweed from green and red pipe-cleaners and stick them to the floor of the aquarium. Stick some fish to the seaweed. Paint some shells in bright colours and stick these on the bottom.

NEWSCASTER MAKE-UP TIPS
Sponge a little red paint on your cheeks and paint on a moustache to match your hair.

DIVER COSTUME TIPS
Wear some Bermuda shorts, colourful flippers, snorkel and mask, and a rubber ring. If it's a cold day, wear black leggings or tights and a black polo-neck jumper with a yellow belt to look like a wet suit.

9

GLOBE HEADS

Bowl everyone over with these crazy costumes. You will find the party goes swimmingly right up until it's time for tea.

FISH BOWL

YOU WILL NEED: Old newspapers; water; flour; bowl and wooden spoon; 1.5 m of flowery material; blue, yellow and pink paint; green and brown pipe-cleaners; orange card; black felt-tip pen; pipe lagging; large square of stiff card; large balloon; sticky tape; 30 cm of thin wire; pencil; glue; craft knife; scissors.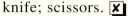

1 Blow up a large balloon. Gradually mix some flour and water in a bowl to make a paste. Tear the newspapers into small strips, dip them into the paste and stick them to the balloon. Cover the balloon with two layers of paper and leave to dry. Do this four times, then burst the balloon and remove it.

2 Cut a hole in the bottom of the papier mâché ball for your head to go through and one in the front for your face. Cut off the top and glue pipe lagging around the hole to make the rim of the bowl. Paint the top of the bowl blue, the bottom yellow and the rim pink.

MAKE-UP TIPS
Paint fish and weed on your cheeks for the fish bowl, and a flower for the teapot.

COSTUME TIPS
For the fish bowl and the teapot, wear a one-piece dance costume, or leggings and a matching top. Choose a colour to match the rest of your outfit.

TEAPOT PROP TIPS

Take a large cup with you to the party and pretend to pour tea into it for your friends.

3 Cut out fish shapes from orange card and draw on some details with a black felt-tip pen. Wrap green and brown pipe-cleaners around a pencil, then stretch them out slightly. Stick the pipe-cleaners and all but one of the fish to the bowl.

4 Stick the last fish to a piece of wire. Wrap the wire around a pencil to make it into a spiral. Stick the wire to the inside of the bowl so that the fish looks as if it were jumping out of the bowl.

TEAPOT

Follow the instructions for the fish bowl to make a papier mâché bowl. Cut a hole in the front and bottom but not in the top. Paint the bowl white and stick on felt flowers and leaves. Draw around the top to mark the lid and add a plastic knob on top. Cut a spout and handle shape from stiff white card. Cut slits in either side of the teapot into which you can push the handle and spout – two slits for the handle and one large one for the spout. Stick the teapot to a table in the same way as the fish bowl.

5 Cover a square of stiff card with material, letting it hang down on all sides like a tablecloth. Cut a hole in the middle for your head to go through, slightly larger than the hole in the bowl. Put the bowl in the hole and tape the edges to the underside of the card.

WINTER WONDERS

What could be better for a Christmas party than a colourful Christmas tree and a large fluffy snowman?

CHRISTMAS TREE

YOU WILL NEED: 6 m of pipe lagging; 3 m of bright-green cotton material; 3 m of dark-green netting; 3 m of bright-green netting; 3 m of sparkly green organza; Christmas tree decorations; sticky tape; needle and thread; 2 m of strong cotton; coat-hanger; scissors.

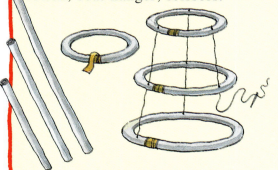

3 Hang the frame on a coat-hanger. Wrap green cotton around the frame. Fold it over the top and bottom hoops and sew it in place. Put on the costume and ask a friend to mark where your arms go, then cut out the armholes.

1 Cut three lengths of lagging – one 1.5 m long, one 2 m long and one 2.5 m long. Bend each piece into a circle and tape the ends together.

2 Tie a knot in the end of the cotton and push it through the smallest hoop of lagging. Tie another knot in the cotton underneath the lagging. Push the cotton through the middle hoop and through the large hoop. Leave 60 cm of cotton between each hoop and tie a knot in the cotton underneath each one. Link the hoops like this in two other places to make a frame.

4 Wrap dark-green netting around the costume in a spiral and secure it with stitches. Do the same with some bright-green netting and green organza. Sew on Christmas decorations.

TREE HAT

Cut a circle of card 50 cm across. Cut a slit from the edge to the middle, roll the card into a cone and tape the edges together. Attach some elastic for a chin strap and sew on Christmas decorations to match those on the tree. Cut a star shape from card, cover it with gold material and glue it on the top.

TREE SHOES

Take two shoe boxes and stick their lids down. Cut holes in the top to put your feet through. Cover the boxes with Christmas paper. Cover some small boxes with Christmas paper and stick these to the top of the shoe boxes to look like a pile of presents.

COSTUME AND MAKE-UP TIPS
Wear a polo-neck jumper and tights or leggings. For the tree's make-up, use red on your cheeks and lips. For the snowman, sponge on a white base, then add red cheeks and black lips.

SNOWMAN

YOU WILL NEED: 6 m of pipe lagging; 9 m of wadding; needle and thread; 2 m of strong cotton; black felt; coat-hanger; newspapers; flour; water, bowl and wooden spoon; sticky tape; large balloon; scissors; glue.

1 Make a frame as for the Christmas tree. Cover it with 6 m of wadding. Sew the wadding over the top and bottom hoops. Cut two armholes and stick four black felt circles down the middle of the body for buttons.

2 Cut four pieces of wadding a little longer than your arms and four times wider. Sew them together to form two tubes and sew them into the armholes. Stitch around the cuffs and gather them slightly.

3 Make a papier mâché head (see page 10). Cover the head with wadding and stitch it to the papier mâché to secure it.

HAT AND SCARF

Cut 5 cm slits all along a strip of card, 60 cm by 45 cm, and fold the pieces outward. Put the strip inside a ring of card 30 cm wide and tape the pieces flat underneath. Make similar flaps in a circle of card 40 cm across and fix the circle to the top of the hat. Cover the hat with black felt and decorate it with red and green felt.
Make a stripy scarf by sticking red felt rectangles on a strip of white felt. Add wool tassles. Make a cone from a sheet of orange card. Draw brown lines around it, then sew on elastic to go around your head.

TOY BOX

Spring to life or flop on the floor. Party time is playtime when you choose to be one of these toys.

JACK-IN-THE-BOX

YOU WILL NEED: 2 m of stripy material; 6 m of pipe lagging; 1 m of white cotton material; four big bright buttons; glue; scissors; needle and thread; Velcro; pins; sticky tape.

JACK-IN-THE-BOX MAKE-UP TIPS
Sponge red on your cheeks and blue on your eyelids and around your eyes. Paint your lips red and give yourself 'smile' lines.

1 Cut four lengths of lagging, 1.5 m long. Tape the ends together and make a frame as for the Christmas tree on page 12.

JACK'S BOX

Cut off all but one flap of a large cardboard box. Tape one flap to the remaining flap. Fix ropes to the top of the box to cross over your shoulders. Paint the box blue, then stick red tape around the edges and an A, B, C and D to the sides.

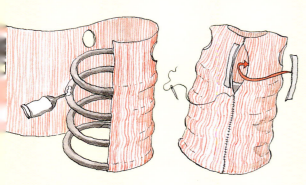

2 Cut some stripy material to reach from the floor to your neck and around the hoops. Stick it to the hoops and cut two armholes. Sew up the back leaving a gap at the top. Sew Velcro into this gap.

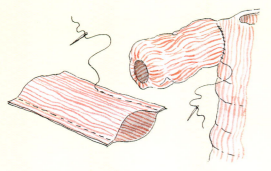

3 Cut four pieces of fabric a little longer than your arms and three times wider. Sew them together, right side inside. Turn the tubes right side outside and sew them into the armholes.

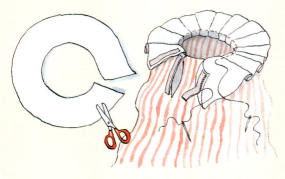

4 Make a ruff from a 60 cm circle of white cotton. Cut in from the edge, then cut out a 3 cm circle from the middle. Pin the cotton inside the neck of the stripy tube, gathering it to fit. Sew it in place and sew Velcro to the ends.

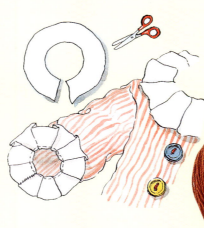

5 Make cuffs in the same way as the ruff, but sew the ends together. Sew four big buttons down the front of the costume.

JACK-IN-THE-BOX COSTUME TIPS
Most of you will be covered by the stripy tube, but wear some long gloves to match it. Wear a bright curly wig too.

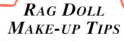

RAG DOLL MAKE-UP TIPS
Sponge red on your cheeks and green on your eyelids, then paint in long black eyelashes and arched eyebrows. Paint your lips red.

RAG DOLL

Cut some squares from check material and sew them to an old long dress using thick thread so it shows. Make a wig from an old cap and some thick wool. Cut the peak off the cap and stick lengths of wool over the cap. Cut the fringe short, split the rest of the hair in half and tie it in bunches. Wear stripy tights and a short sleeved shirt if your dress is sleeveless.

FRUIT BOWL

These fruity costumes will make you the pick of the bunch at any party. Ask a friend to dress up in one of the costumes and you can go out together as a fruit salad.

BUNCH OF GRAPES

YOU WILL NEED: Two packs of different-sized purple balloons; newspapers; water; flour; bowl and wooden spoon; thick card; green paint; green crêpe paper; wire; elastic; glue; sticky tape; scissors; craft knife. ✗

1 Blow up a small balloon. Cover the top with papier mâché (see page 10) to make a cap.

2 Cut a slit in the cap. Push in a stalk made from card, and paint the cap and stalk green. Fix elastic to go under your chin.

3 Wrap green crêpe paper around several lengths of wire, gluing it as you go. Bend the wires into spiral shapes, push them through the hat and tape them to the inside.

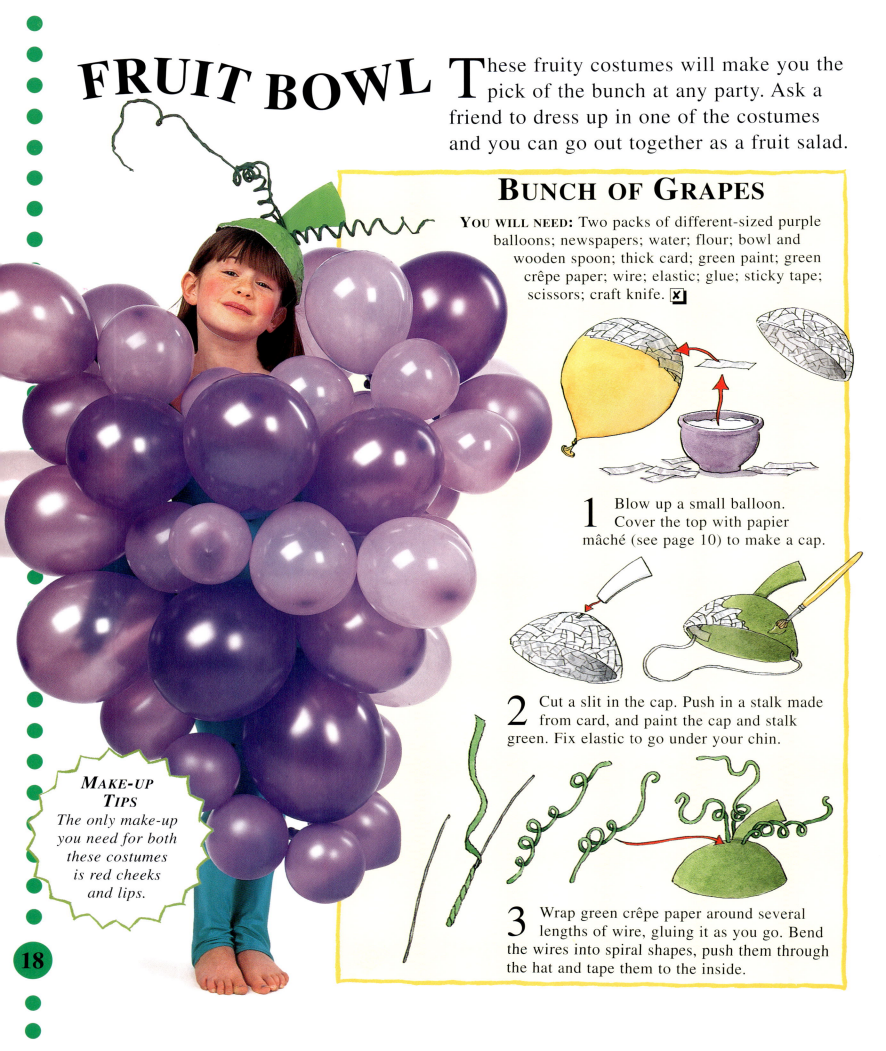

BANANA

YOU WILL NEED: Four strips of pale-coloured foam, 2 m by 50 cm; yellow craft spray; 7 m of brown ribbon; A2 sheet of white card; 1 m of wadding; 50 cm of pale-yellow cotton material; needle and thread; glue; scissors. ☒

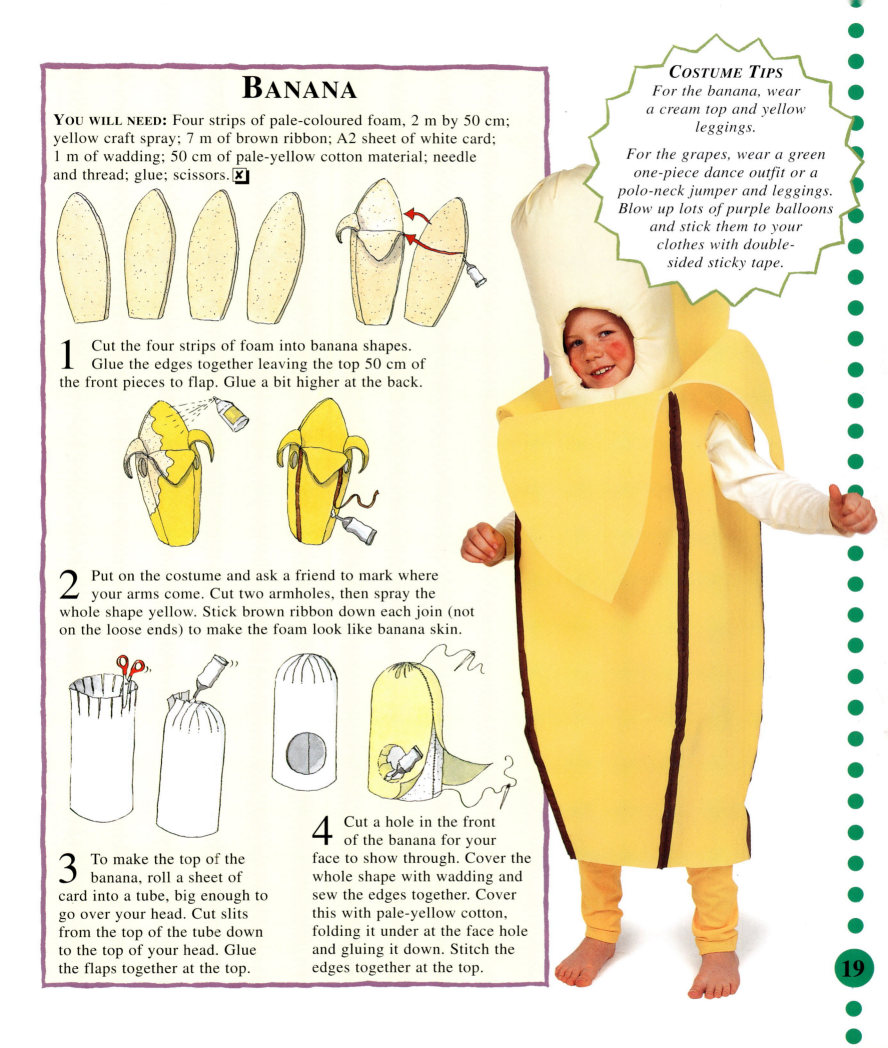

1 Cut the four strips of foam into banana shapes. Glue the edges together leaving the top 50 cm of the front pieces to flap. Glue a bit higher at the back.

2 Put on the costume and ask a friend to mark where your arms come. Cut two armholes, then spray the whole shape yellow. Stick brown ribbon down each join (not on the loose ends) to make the foam look like banana skin.

3 To make the top of the banana, roll a sheet of card into a tube, big enough to go over your head. Cut slits from the top of the tube down to the top of your head. Glue the flaps together at the top.

4 Cut a hole in the front of the banana for your face to show through. Cover the whole shape with wadding and sew the edges together. Cover this with pale-yellow cotton, folding it under at the face hole and gluing it down. Stitch the edges together at the top.

COSTUME TIPS

For the banana, wear a cream top and yellow leggings.

For the grapes, wear a green one-piece dance outfit or a polo-neck jumper and leggings. Blow up lots of purple balloons and stick them to your clothes with double-sided sticky tape.

STATUES

Y ou don't have to be ancient to dress up as these Roman statues. 'Caesar' the opportunity to 'empress' all your friends.

ROMAN PILLAR

YOU WILL NEED: Piece of foam large enough to reach from the floor to your waist and to go around you in a cylinder shape; two pieces of foam, 45 cm square; two pieces of foam, 35 cm square; grey spray paint; black felt-tip pen; 3 m of washing line; 1 sq m of shiny white material; glue; pencil; scissors; safety pins. ☒

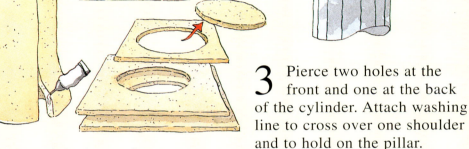

1 Bend the large piece of foam into a cylinder shape and glue the edges together. Draw around one end of the cylinder in the middle of each of the foam squares and cut out the circles.

2 Glue one small square on top of each big square. Glue one of these shapes around each end of the cylinder and spray the whole pillar grey. When it is dry, draw black lines down the pillar.

3 Pierce two holes at the front and one at the back of the cylinder. Attach washing line to cross over one shoulder and to hold on the pillar.

4 Spray the white material grey in patches, blending them in to the white. Wrap this over one shoulder to cover the washing line and pin it at the back.

IVY

Wrap strips of green crêpe paper around a long piece of garden wire, gluing them down. Cut some ivy leaf shapes from green card and stick to the wire. Wrap it around you for both the pillar costume and the bronze statue.

PILLAR HEAD-DRESS

Bend some wire into a circle to fit around your head with a bit extra. Bend the extra bit around the circle of wire to secure it. Cut small leaf shapes from green card and stick them to the wire, all facing the same way and slightly overlapping. Repeat until the whole circle is covered.

BRONZE STATUE PROP TIPS

Hold a bronze bowl of fruit on the flat of one hand. Make the bowl from an old plastic bowl. Almost fill the bowl with wadding and place some fake fruit on top. Spray the whole thing bronze. ❌

MAKE-UP TIPS

For the pillar, sponge dark grey, pale grey and white body paint over all the parts of your body that show, including your lips and ears.

For the bronze statue, sponge terracotta body paint all over. Sponge a little bronze glitter gel over your face and hair.

BRONZE STATUE

Make the head-dress in the same way as the pillar head-dress, then spray it bronze. ❌ For the dress, hem a large piece of bronze-coloured material. Wrap it around your body and under both arms. Pin it securely under one arm and throw the extra piece of material over your shoulder and pin it at the back.

21

SWEET SHOP

If you want to mix well with everyone at the party, get wrapped up in one of these stripy costumes. You'll look as sweet as candy.

BOILED SWEET

YOU WILL NEED: Large roll of stripy wrapping paper; two pillowcases; wadding; 2 m of Cellophane wrapping; 1 m of Velcro; stapler; needle and thread; sticky tape; scissors. ☒

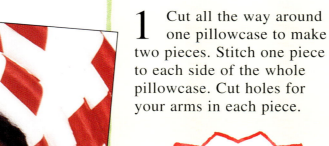

1 Cut all the way around one pillowcase to make two pieces. Stitch one piece to each side of the whole pillowcase. Cut holes for your arms in each piece.

2 Stuff the pillow case with wadding and sew up the top. Cover the whole shape with stripy wrapping paper, securing it with staples. Sew Velcro to the separate pieces to do up at the back.

MAKE-UP AND COSTUME TIPS
*A one-piece dance ou*f*it is best for both of these costumes, or leggings and a polo-neck jumper. Sew sweets all over the arms and legs. Keep your make-up simple and give yourself pink cheeks and lips.*

3 Carefully wrap the sweet in Cellophane with about 50 cm extra at each end. Put sticky tape around the Cellophane at each end of the sweet to make it look like twisted sweet paper. Cut the Cellophane at the armholes, wrap it inside and secure it with staples. Cut the Cellophane at the top so your face shows through.

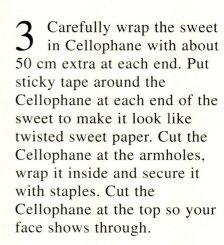

22

LOLLIPOP

Wind some pipe lagging into a spiral, leaving a hole in the middle for your face. Tape the spiral across the back to hold it together, then paint the whole shape white. When it is dry, stick on small pieces of red tape to make the stripes. Use the cardboard inside of a large roll of wrapping paper for a stick and paint it brown. Cut a hole in the bottom of the spiral and push the stick into it. Make a large red crêpe bow and stick it to the front.

23

SUMMER SPECIALS

Whether you are a bright sunflower or a shining sun, you will look perfect at a summer party.

SUNFLOWER

YOU WILL NEED: Stiff card; thin yellow card; orange crêpe paper; Velcro; scissors; glue.

SUNFLOWER COSTUME TIPS

Make a spiky green felt collar to look like leaves. Cut two flowerpots from terracotta-coloured card. Stick brown felt with a wavy edge inside the top of the flowerpots and wear the whole shape with a pair of bright braces. Wear a bright-green, long-sleeved top, brown tights and wellies. Carry a watering can wound around with ivy (see page 20).

SUNFLOWER MAKE-UP TIPS

Sponge a bright yellow base all over your face, then blend in red cheeks. Paint a green leaf shape above each eye and paint your lips red.

SUN

Make a band of card (see sunflower above). Cut out eight sun rays from red and yellow card. Also cut out gold card triangles. Stick them inside the band of card and fold them back. Add a circle of orange sun to the front, a blue sky behind and some white clouds.

SUNFLOWER PROP TIPS

Cut a polystyrene ball in half. Paint it red with a black head and spots to look like a ladybird. Glue it to one of the yellow petals.

1 Cut a strip of card 6 cm wide and long enough to go around your face. Glue Velcro to the ends so that you can join the strip under your chin.

2 Cut out some petals from yellow card, 26 cm long. Fold over 6 cm and glue the fold to the inside of the ring of card. (Cut out several petals at a time by folding the card a few times and cutting through all the layers at once.)

3 Cut a strip of orange crêpe paper, 14 cm by 30 cm. Fold over 1 cm at one end, then fold back 1 cm. Fold backwards and forwards to the end of the strip. Stick it around the inside of the petal ring and fold it over the front of the flower.

SUN COSTUME TIPS
Wear a bright blue shirt. You could stick on some kites, birds, clouds, a rainbow or even an aeroplane.

SUN MAKE-UP TIPS
Sponge a yellow base all over your face and blend in red on your cheeks. Paint red and orange rays above your eyes and over your forehead and add some glitter to make you shine. Paint your lips red with extra 'smile' lines.

25

BARMY BOXES

D ress up as a clock or the princess in the tower, and you'll have the time of your life.

CLOCK

YOU WILL NEED: Long narrow cardboard box; square cardboard box; card; fake wood sticky-back plastic; gold doilies; gold braid; a small door knob; scissors; glue.

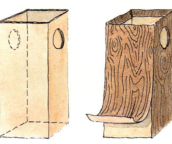

1 Cut the flaps off a long cardboard box and cut out two armholes. Cover it with fake wood plastic.

2 Cut a piece of card slightly smaller than the front of the long box and cover this with fake wood plastic. Stick gold braid all the way around, about 1 cm in from the edge. Stick on the door knob, then glue the whole piece to the front of the body of the clock.

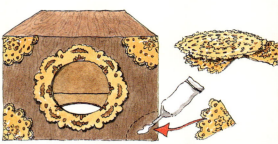

3 Cut a hole in the bottom of a square box for your head to go through and a hole in the front for your face. Cover the box with fake wood plastic and decorate with gold doilies.

4 Cut some card into a curvy shape and decorate it with braid and doilies. Glue two pieces of card to the back so that they extend below and push them into two matching slits in the top of the clock. Stick the top of the clock to the body.

COSTUME TIPS

For the clock, wear a brown or yellow top and leggings or tights.

For the princess, wear a long dress with long sleeves. You could look for one in a second-hand shop. Dress it up with a cotton-wool collar and cuffs. Wear a gold necklace and a thick gold belt.

MAKE-UP TIPS

For the clock, sponge white over your face. Paint on black clock numbers and red hands on your nose.

For the princess, dab some red on your cheeks and paint your lips pink.

PRINCESS'S TOWER

PRINCESS'S HAT

Cut a circle of card about 50 cm across. Cut a slit from the edge to the middle, bend the card into a cone shape and glue the edges together. Cut off the top of the hat, then cover it with shiny material. Stick velvet around the bottom of the hat. Push some netting into the top so that it hangs down behind.

YOU WILL NEED: Large oblong cardboard box; shallow cardboard box; dark grey paint; grey card; brown card; rope; black felt-tip pen; purple velvet; yellow material; stripy material; gold braid; glue; scissors.

1 Cut off the bottom flaps of a large box and keep them. Bend the top flaps out. Cut a shallow box into a battlement shape and stick it on to the flaps of the large box. Fix two pieces of rope to the battlements from back to front to go over your shoulders. Paint the boxes grey.

2 Cut brick shapes from grey card and stick them to the tower. Cut a door from brown card. Draw on a black keyhole and lines to look like wood, then stick it to the tower.

3 Take the flaps that you cut off the large box and cut a triangle out of one end of each. Cover the flaps with stripy material and stick them to hang down from the battlements as pennants.

4 Make a card pennant, about twice as big as the first two. Cover it with purple velvet. Cut out a dragon from yellow material and stick it on the velvet. Trim the pennant with gold braid and stick it to the front of the tower.

27

FIREWORKS

Make the party go with a bang and dress up as a sparkly Catherine wheel or Roman candle.

CATHERINE WHEEL

YOU WILL NEED: A1 piece of stiff card; A2 piece of silver card; 4 m of rope; green, yellow, orange, blue, pink and silver crêpe paper; thin wire; 4 m of thin washing line; scissors; glue; sticky tape.

1 Cut a circle of card from an A1 sheet, big enough to cover most of you. Make four small holes 25 cm in from the side and 25 cm in from the top and bottom. Attach two pieces of washing line to make straps to cross over your shoulders.

2 Starting in the middle, spiral the rope over the card leaving a space between the circles. Glue it down as you go. Glue lengths of green, yellow, orange, blue and pink crêpe paper inside the spiral.

3 Cut a piece of silver crêpe paper, 40 cm by 60 cm. Fold this like a concertina and cut points along one end. Cut the remaining silver crêpe paper into long strips 10 cm wide. Glue these to the rope all along the spiral and glue the concertina to the bottom of the wheel.

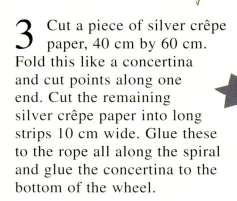

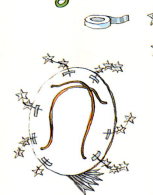

4 Cut stars from silver card. Stick them to lengths of wire using sticky tape. Stick these to the back of the Catherine wheel.

MAKE-UP TIPS
For the Catherine wheel, sponge on pink cheeks. Give yourself pink lips and decorate your face with glittery silver gel.

For the Roman candle, just give yourself some pink cheeks.

28

ROMAN CANDLE'S HAT

Cut out a card circle, 30 cm across. Cut a slit to the middle, make a cone and cover with silver paper. Stick shiny stars to wires, push them into the cone and tape them down inside.

COSTUME TIPS
Wear a one-piece dance outfit of a suitable colour to go with your firework, or leggings and a polo-neck jumper.

ROMAN CANDLE

YOU WILL NEED: Two A1 pieces of yellow card; pink, green, dark-blue and pale-blue crêpe paper; glue; sticky tape; scissors.

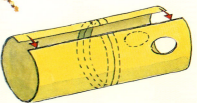

1 Tape two pieces of card together. Bend them to form a cylinder and tape the edges. Cut two armholes.

2 Cut different width pieces of pink, green and dark-blue crêpe paper, long enough to go around the cylinder at an angle. Glue them on.

3 Unfold some pale-blue crêpe paper. Glue one edge all the way around inside the top of the cylinder, gathering it together as you go.

29

MERMAID

Y ou do not have to go to the sea to be this mermaid. Go to a party and you'll have some fishy tales to tell.

MERMAID'S ROCK

YOU WILL NEED: 4 m of netting, wide enough to reach from your waist to the ground; 3 m of silver material; green crêpe paper; 8 large shells; different bright-coloured paint; safety pin; 40 cm of elastic; needle and thread; glue; scissors.

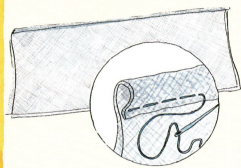

1 Fold the netting in half lengthways. Fold over 3 cm of the folded edge and sew it all the way along to form a tube.

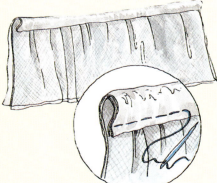

2 Cover the front of the netting with silver material. Fold about 3 cm over the tube of netting at the top and sew it down, keeping the tube of netting open.

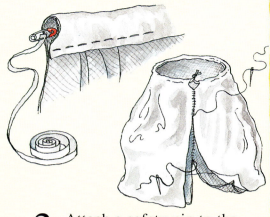

3 Attach a safety pin to the end of a length of elastic and thread it through the tube. Tie the ends together to fit your waist. Sew together the edges of the netting and the silver material to form a full skirt.

4 Shred some crêpe paper and sew it to the skirt in bunches to look like seaweed. Paint some shells in bright colours and stick them to the skirt when they are dry.

MERMAID'S HAIR

Cut the peak off an old cap and glue long strips of yellow crêpe paper all over the cap for hair. Cut a fringe and make the bottom of the hair even all around.

MERMAID'S OUTFIT

Cut two shell shapes from card to cover your chest and two identical shapes from silver lamé. Cut the lamé into sections and stick them to the card. Make a chest band with shoulder straps using elastic covered with green sequins and stick the shells to the front. Sew Velcro to the ends of the band.

30

MERMAID'S TAIL

YOU WILL NEED: An old pair of cycling shorts, trousers, or pants; 1 m of green lamé; 1 m of silver lamé; thin foam, wide enough to wrap half way around you and long enough to go from your waist to the floor; another piece of foam 40 cm square; glue; card; scissors; pencil; needle and thread.

1 Cut out a fish shape from foam. Draw just around the tail on the other piece of foam and cut it out. Cut this shape into five sections.

2 Make a scale shape from card. Draw around this several times on green and silver lamé to make enough scales to cover one side of the tail. Glue the scales to the tail in overlapping rows of alternate colours.

3 Cover the five foam tail sections with green and silver lamé and stick them on the main tail. Sew the tail to the waistband of your shorts. Place tail over the top of the Mermaid's Rock.

MAKE-UP TIPS
Sponge red on your cheeks and paint your lips red. Give yourself a large arch of rainbow colours above each eye.

PROPS AND ACCESSORIES
Make a mirror from card with small shells stuck on the back. Paint the back silver and stick silver foil to the front. For the hair band, stick shells to an Alice band and paint it silver. Wear a necklace of seashell shapes.

OLD MASTERS

Y̶ou will really look a picture when you dress up as one of these framed masterpieces.

PICASSO FRAME

Make two frames out of white card, in the same way as for the laughing cavalier, but make them the same size. Stick the frames together and cover the front with irregular-shaped pieces of coloured card.

PICASSO FRAME COSTUME TIPS
Wear a one-piece dance outfit, or leggings and a top. Pin on some coloured card shapes to match the frame.

LAUGHING CAVALIER

YOU WILL NEED: Two pieces of stiff gold card, 150 cm by 120 cm; four pots of gold glitter; gold braid; pencil; scissors; ruler; newspaper; glue.

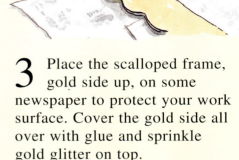

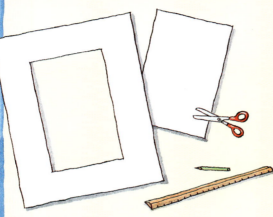

1 Draw a rectangle 60 cm by 90 cm in the middle of the back of one piece of card, leaving 60 cm all around. Cut out the rectangle and keep the frame.

2 Make another frame from the other piece of card, but make the rectangle larger than before so that the frame is about 8 cm smaller all around than the first. Give this frame a scalloped edge and pointed corners as shown.

3 Place the scalloped frame, gold side up, on some newspaper to protect your work surface. Cover the gold side all over with glue and sprinkle gold glitter on top.

4 When the glue is dry, stick the scalloped frame on top of the larger frame. Glue braid all around the scalloped edge.

CAVALIER COSTUME TIPS

As the cavalier, wear red leggings or tights, riding or wellington boots, a white frilly shirt and a waistcoat. Add some gold braid and buttons to the waistcoat. Give yourself a sash by wrapping a long piece of material over one shoulder and pinning the ends together at your waist. Wear a cavalier's hat and carry a plastic sword. Drape a large pair of gloves or gauntlets over the frame for the finishing touch.

MAKE-UP TIPS

Give the cavalier a beard, moustache and thick eyebrows using black, brown and ginger-coloured make-up.

For the Picasso face, sponge on a pale blue base and add red cheeks. Give your lips and eyes a black outline, draw high black eyebrows and a stripe down your nose.

OPPOSITES

If you can't decide what to wear, you can dress half-and-half.

BLACK AND WHITE

Find an old waistcoat, T-shirt, cap, trousers, and boots – preferably white or black. Make one half of the clothes black and the other half white with emulsion paint. If you like, you can paint spots on some things. Paint whatever you like on your face as long as it is black and white. You could have dots, squares, or stripes. Use face paints to make your lips black and white too.

DAY AND NIGHT

YOU WILL NEED: 1.5 m of pale-blue cotton material; 1.5 m of dark-blue cotton material; 50 cm of dark-brown cotton material; 50 cm of green cotton material; 2 m of different brown material; 50 cm each of red, dark-blue, white, dark-brown, light-brown, pink, grey, black and yellow felt; silver card; silver sequins; 1 m of wadding; A2 sheet of card; fishing wire; plastic bats and butterflies; needle and thread; gold braid; cotton wool; glue; scissors.

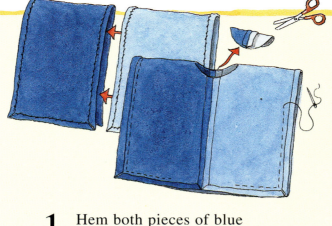

1 Hem both pieces of blue cotton. Fold them in half inside out and sew them together. Cut a hole in the middle of the folds for your head to go through, then sew all the edges together to form a big bag. Leave a gap at the bottom so that you can get into the bag. Turn the bag the right way out.

2 Cut a strip of wadding as tall as the bag and 50 cm wide for the tree. Cover it with brown material, sticking it around the back to secure it. Cut two hill shapes from wadding. Cover one with dark-brown cotton and one with green cotton. Stick the hills and the tree to the bag.

3 Glue on a branch of brown material. Make a sun, moon, rabbit, mouse, owl and flowers from felt and stick them in position. Make the rabbit's tail with cotton wool. Cut silver stars from card and stick these around the moon. Sew silver sequins in between. Stick gold braid around the sun as rays.

4 Roll a sheet of card into a tube that fits over your head. Stick the edges of the tube together and cut a hole in the front for your face. Cut a jagged edge at the top of the trunk. Cut two pieces of card to make branches and cover the trunk and the branches with brown material. Cut a slit in either side of the trunk and push in the branches. Attach fishing wire to plastic butterflies and bats, and attach these to the branches.

MAKE-UP AND COSTUME TIPS

Sponge red on your cheeks. You can wear what you like because it will not show, but if your neck shows, wear a brown polo-neck jumper.

35

VEGETABLE SOUP

A garden party would be a good occasion to get 'souped up' as a vegetable. It will be a recipe for success.

CARROT

YOU WILL NEED: Sheet of A1 stiff card; wadding to cover the card; orange cotton material to cover the card; 5 m of brown ribbon; green crêpe paper; fishing wire; 25 cm of elastic; 3 m of washing line; sticky tape; wire cutters; glue; scissors. ☒

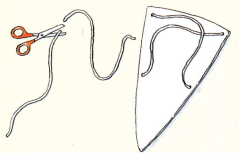

1 Cut out a carrot shape from card to reach from your chin nearly to the floor. Fix two pieces of washing line to the carrot to cross over your back and hold on the costume.

2 Cut a piece of wadding slightly larger than the card. Stick it to the front, gluing the edges around the back. Do the same with orange cotton. Stick lengths of brown ribbon across the carrot.

3 Cut a circle 30 cm across from card. Cut a slit in it from the edge to the middle, bend it around to form a cone to fit on your head. Glue the edges together. Cover the cone with green crêpe paper, and attach elastic to go under your chin.

4 Cut lengths of wire, some 45 cm long and others 30 cm. Cut pieces of crêpe paper the same length and 15 cm wide. Fold the paper in half and stick wires inside the folds. Snip the paper to form tassles. Tape the wires together at one end to form a bunch of leaves. Stick them through the top of the hat, securing them inside with tape.

MAKE-UP TIPS
For the carrot, give yourself rosy cheeks.

For the pea pod, paint your face and neck green. Add brown cheeks and green lips.

PEA POD

YOU WILL NEED: 5 m of green material; two pieces of foam, a little bit taller than you and double the width; 30 sq cm of green felt; A2 sheet of silver card; Velcro; needle and thread; thick green thread; glue; scissors.

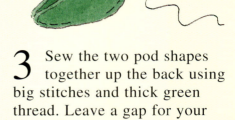

1 Cut two pea pod shapes from foam. Mark where your arms will go – one through each piece – and cut holes.

2 Cut four pod shapes from green material, slightly larger than the foam shapes. (Use one foam piece as a guide.) Put one piece of foam between two pieces of material. Cut through the armholes and sew all the edges together.

3 Sew the two pod shapes together up the back using big stitches and thick green thread. Leave a gap for your legs to go through.

4 Cut strips of silver card, 5 cm by 5 cm. Glue them around the front edges of the pod as a zip. Make a puller for the zip from silver card and stick it to the edge of one piece of the pod. Sew Velcro inside the zip from the puller to the bottom.

5 Cut a circle of green felt, large enough to fit around the top of the pod. Cut it into points. Roll another piece of felt, 30 cm by 8 cm, into a tube and glue it to the middle of the circle as a stalk. Glue the stalk to the top of the pod.

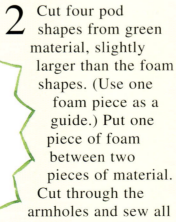

COSTUME TIPS

For the pea pod, wear green leggings or tights and a green long-sleeved, polo-neck jumper. Blow up some green balloons and stick them to the front of your top to look like peas.

For the carrot, wear brown tights with a long-sleeved top and shorts.

CRAZY KITCHEN

You will not be left out in the cold when you wear one of these kitchen creations. Spin into the room at the party and you'll turn the atmosphere electric.

FRIDGE

Make the basic box as for the washing machine but do not cut a hole in the front. Cover it with white sticky-back plastic. Make a door from card, cover it with sticky-back plastic and stick it to the fridge with thick, silver sticky tape. Put silver sticky tape along all the edges and across the door and front of the fridge as shelves. Make food from card and paper, and stick it to the fridge.

PLANT POT

Cut a flowerpot shape from terracotta-coloured card and cut a hole in the front for your face. Make some leaves from green material and stick these to the back of the pot so that they fall over the top. Fold under the bottom of the pot and glue it onto the fridge.

WASHING MACHINE

YOU WILL NEED: Large square cardboard box; large roll of white sticky-back plastic; two plastic bottle lids; round see-through plastic cake packaging; old bits of material or clothing; thick card; glue; large sticky dots; black felt; silver craft spray; scissors; black felt-tip pen. ☒

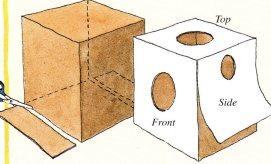

1 Cut off the flaps at one end of a cardboard box. Stick the other end securely and cut a hole in it for your head. Cut two armholes in the sides, and a hole in the front, 30 cm across. Cover the whole shape with white sticky-back plastic.

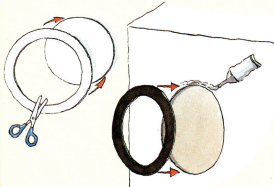

2 Cut a 5 cm ring of card. Cover the ring with black felt and stick it around the hole in the front of the machine.

SOAP PACKET

Cut off the front of a cereal packet and cut a hole for your face. Paint it to look like a packet of soap powder and glue it to the washing machine.

3 Cut another ring of card the same size and spray it silver. Stick it to the cake packaging to make the door. Cut a triangle of thick card and glue the top to the left-hand side of the black ring. Glue the door to the bottom of the triangle.

4 Cut a small rectangle of card and cover it with sticky-back plastic. Stick on some dots, then stick the card to the machine. Outline it using the black felt-tip pen. Glue some old bits of material and clothing inside the machine. Stick on some bottle lids as knobs.

MAKE-UP AND
COSTUME TIPS
*For both outfits, sponge
red on your cheeks and
paint your lips red.
Wear black tights and
a black polo-neck
jumper.*

SPACE FRONTIERS

Launch out and be different. You'll be over the Moon when you see yourself in one of these costumes.

ALIEN

YOU WILL NEED: 4 m of shiny green material; string of silver stars; bubble wrap; A2 sheet of orange card; newspapers; water; flour; bowl and wooden spoon; large pear-shaped balloon; green craft spray; 6 colourful table-tennis balls; glue; needle and thread; scissors; craft knife. ✗

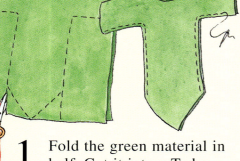

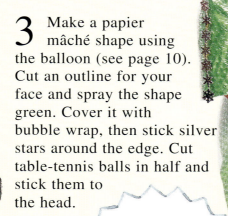

1 Fold the green material in half. Cut it into a T-shape with the fold along the top. Cut a hole for your neck in the middle of the fold. Cut the bottom of the material into a point, then sew up the edges to make a long-sleeved dress.

3 Make a papier mâché shape using the balloon (see page 10). Cut an outline for your face and spray the shape green. Cover it with bubble wrap, then stick silver stars around the edge. Cut table-tennis balls in half and stick them to the head.

2 Cover the dress in bubble wrap, gluing it down. Stick a string of silver stars down the sleeves and in a point around the neck. Make an alien symbol out of orange card and glue it to the front of the dress.

ALIEN COSTUME TIPS
Wear grey or green leggings, or tights and a polo-neck jumper.

ALIEN MAKE-UP TIPS
Sponge green all over your face. Add white arched eyebrows and lips. Outline your eyes, eyebrows and lips in black.

ROCKET

YOU WILL NEED: Sheet of silver card, large enough to go around you and reach from the floor to the top of your head; 2 pieces of A1 red card; sticky-back, red hologram paper; piece of very stiff card, about 30 cm square; piece of gold material, about 35 cm square; pack of gold drawing pins; orange, yellow and red crêpe paper; glue; scissors; craft knife. ✗

ROCKET MAKE-UP AND COSTUME TIPS
Wear a grey or silver top with leggings, or a grey one-piece dance outfit. Sponge red on your cheeks.

1 Roll the silver card into a tube that just fits around you and stick it together at the edges. Cut two armholes and a hole for your face. Cut some pointed strips of crêpe paper and stick these inside the bottom of the tube as flames.

2 Cut a circle of red card about 60 cm across. Cut a slit to the middle and roll it into a cone, sticking the edges together with glue. Cover the cone with red hologram paper and stick it to the top of the tube.

3 Cut two fins 10 cm by 10 cm, and a rectangle, 60 cm by 40 cm, from red card. Cover them with red hologram paper. Cut a slit in each side of the rocket for the fins. Stick the rectangle to the front.

4 Cut a circle, 30 cm across, from stiff card. Cut out a circle from the middle, 25 cm across, leaving a ring 5 cm wide. Cover the ring with gold material and stick in drawing pins all the way around. Ask an adult to cut off any points inside the rocket.

41

WILD RIDERS

Get ready, keep steady and go to the party on horseback. You'll have a galloping good time.

KNIGHT

YOU WILL NEED: 2 m of red cotton material; 50 cm of white felt; yellow felt; 2 m of silver netting; needle and thread; glue; pencil; scissors.

1 Fold the red material in half. Lie on it and ask a friend to draw around you from your neck to your thighs. Get up and draw in the neck line and along the bottom. Cut out the shape through both halves of the material. Cut off the arms and sew the two shapes together up the sides and across the shoulders, leaving the neck and arms open.

2 Cut out four pieces of silver netting a little wider and longer than your arms. Sew the pieces together in pairs leaving the ends open. Sew these arms into the armholes, then turn the tunic inside-out.

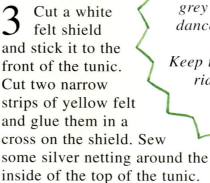

3 Cut a white felt shield and stick it to the front of the tunic. Cut two narrow strips of yellow felt and glue them in a cross on the shield. Sew some silver netting around the inside of the top of the tunic.

KNIGHT'S HELMET

Use a box big enough to fit over your head. Try to find a hexagonal box (or use a small square box). Cut the flaps off one end and cut a hole in the front for your face. Paint the helmet silver, then stick some long feathers in the top.

COSTUME AND MAKE-UP TIPS
For the knight, wear a grey or silver one-piece dance outfit, or leggings and a top.
Keep the make-up for both riders simple – just sponge on red cheeks.

HOBBY HORSE

YOU WILL NEED: A2 piece of white card; grey card; small piece of white felt; small piece of black felt; sheet of gold card; long broom handle; glue; scissors; blue curtain trim.

RACING JOCKEY

Make the hobby horse as above, but choose different colours and don't put trim on the reins. Wear a riding cap covered with a colourful silk, a bright jersey, breeches, riding boots and gloves, and carry a whip.

1 Cut two horse's head shapes from the white card and two ear shapes. For the mane, cut a curved piece from the grey card, 12 cm wide and as long as the horse's neck. Glue it in position on one of the heads. Cut the card lots of times from the top to the head to make it look like a mane.

2 Glue the two horse heads together with the mane in between them. Leave a hole at the bottom for the broom handle, then glue the handle in place. Glue an ear to each side of the head.

3 Cut two large oval shapes from the white felt and two smaller black ones. Glue them on the head as eyes. Glue on two black felt nostrils. Cut two strips of gold card and glue them on as a bridle and reins. Stick curtain trim on the reins.

43

FESTIVE FANCIES

Be the surprise package at the party in either of these costumes. Choose different colours if you like. If you want to be a cracker for any occasion, not just for Christmas, make up another decoration for the front instead of holly.

CHRISTMAS CRACKER

YOU WILL NEED: Two A1 sheets of card; 2 m of shiny red material; 2 packets of gold crêpe paper; shiny red crêpe paper; white doilies; 2 m of gold ribbon; 2 table-tennis balls; red paint; shiny green paper; glue; scissors.

1 Bend two sheets of card to form a cylinder big enough to go around you. Tape the edges together and trim it so that it reaches from your neck to your shins. Cut armholes and cover the whole shape with shiny red material.

2 Glue two pieces of gold ribbon around the cracker. Fold gold crêpe paper into a 'concertina'. Open it out slightly and stick it around the bottom inside edge of the cracker. Glue a similar piece of gold crêpe paper around the top edge like a collar.

CRACKER MAKE-UP AND COSTUME TIPS
Sponge red on your cheeks, then paint on a sprig of holly. Add some glitter for sparkle. Wear a green one-piece dance outfit or polo-neck jumper and leggings.

PRESENT MAKE-UP AND COSTUME TIPS
Sponge a little red on your cheeks and paint your lips red. Wear tights and a long-sleeved polo-neck jumper to match the ribbon on the box and your hat.

3 Cut an oval of gold crêpe paper. Cut strips of shiny red crêpe paper, 15 cm wide. Concertina them and stick them around the gold oval. Cut some white doilies in half and stick them behind the red crêpe paper to form a frill. Stick the whole thing to the front of the cracker.

4 Cut two holly leaves from shiny green paper and stick them to the gold oval. Paint two table-tennis balls red and glue them to the middle of the holly.

PARTY PRESENT

Cut off the bottom flaps of a large cardboard box. Cut a hole for your head in the other end of the box and an armhole in each side. Cover the box in gold wrapping paper and tape the edges down. Wrap wide, bright-coloured ribbon around the box to finish it off. For the lid, cut out a large square of cardboard and glue a cardboard rim all around the edge. Cut a hole in the middle of the square to fit on your head, then tie on a large ribbon bow.

45